MAKING **HISTORY**

KNIGHTS

Neil Morris and Sue Nicholson

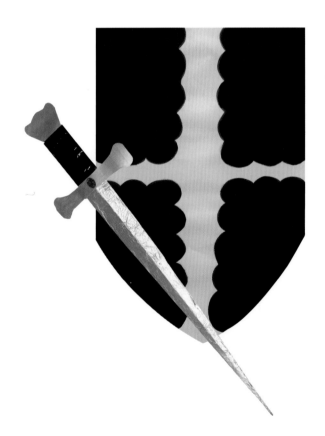

W
FRANKLIN WATTS
LONDON • SYDNEY

First published in 2008 by Franklin Watts

Copyright © Franklin Watts 2008

Franklin Watts
338 Euston Road
London NW1 3BH

Franklin Watts Australia
Level 17/207 Kent Street
Sydney, NSW 2000

A CIP catalogue record for this book is available
from the British Library.

Created by Q2AMedia
Editor: Jean Coppendale
Creative Director: Simmi Sikka
Senior Art Director: Ashita Murgai
Senior Designers: Dibakar Acharjee, Ravijot Singh
Senior Project Manager: Kavita Lad
Project Manager: Gaurav Seth
Picture Researchers: Amit Tigga, Jyoti Sachdeva
Art, Craft & Photography: Tarang Saggar
Illustrators: Amit Tayal, Subash Vohra, Sanyogita Lal
Models: Donagh O' Leary, Ruchi Sharma (hands)

Dewey number: 940.1

ISBN 978 0 7496 7851 7

Note to parents and teachers:
Every effort has been made by the publisher to ensure that the websites in this book are suitable for children, that they
are of the highest educational value, and that they contain no inappropriate or offensive material. However, because of the nature
of the Internet, it is impossible to guarantee that the contents of these sites will not be altered. We strongly advise that Internet
access is supervised by a responsible adult.

Many projects in this book require adult supervision, especially those which involve the use
of scissors and craft knives. Some projects suggest the use of wallpaper paste. It is advised that a fungicide-free
paste (cellulose paste) is used. If in doubt, consult the manufacturer's contents list and instructions. Many projects suggest
the use of paint. It is advised that non-toxic paint is used. If in doubt, consult the manufacturer's contents list and instructions.

Printed in China

Franklin Watts is a division of Hachette Children's Books, an Hachette Livre UK company.

www.hachettelivre.co.uk

Contents

Knights and chivalry

Knights were armoured soldiers who fought during the Middle Ages in Europe. They served their king or a high-ranking nobleman and were trained to fight their lord's enemies on horseback. Many knights became great heroes throughout their land.

Age of chivalry

The Middle Ages is the period between about AD 500 and 1500. After AD 1000, knights developed a code of chivalry. This was a system of behaviour with strict rules and customs. As well as serving their lord, knights were expected to love their country and defend the Church. They also fought evil and injustice. Just as importantly, chivalry meant protecting women, keeping one's word of honour and giving generously to those in need.

A group of 15th-century knights rides ▶ off to battle. One of the lightly armoured knights carries a blue banner. This told others who they were fighting for.

The knight's horses

A knight's horse was his most valuable possession, and he usually had more than one. He rode into battle on a large, powerful warhorse, called a destrier. He often used a sumpter, or packhorse, to carry his equipment to battle.

He rode a well-bred, lighter horse called a palfrey for hunting and long-distance travel. His favourite tournament horse (see page 22) was often a fast charger. A 15th-century writer said that a knight's horse needed special qualities: a man's boldness, a woman's movement, a fox's trot, a hare's eyes and an ass's strong legs. A knight looked after his horses very well.

Levels of society

In the Middle Ages, there were four main classes of society. The monarch was at the very top. Next came noblemen and churchmen. Nobles gained land from the king in exchange for military service. Knights provided this service for their noble lord. Peasants were at the bottom of society. Most worked on the nobleman's land, giving him a large share of the produce. This way of running society is called the feudal system.

Monarch

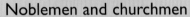

Sceptre: a ceremonial rod of authority

Orb: a ceremonial object showing royalty

King on the royal throne

Noblemen and churchmen

Crosier: a bishop's staff

Baron

Bishop

Knights

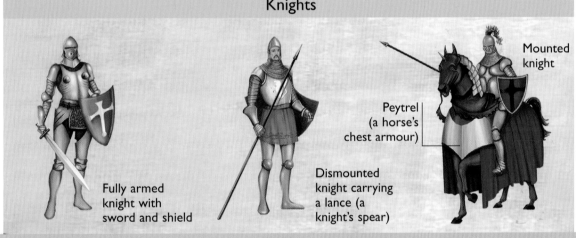

Fully armed knight with sword and shield

Dismounted knight carrying a lance (a knight's spear)

Mounted knight

Peytrel (a horse's chest armour)

Craftsmen, traders and peasants

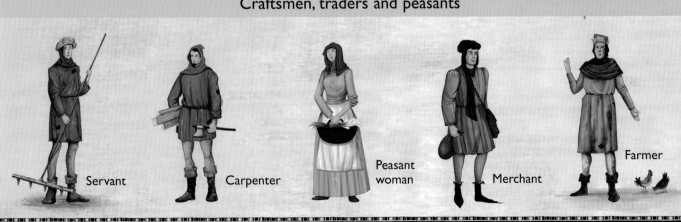

Servant

Carpenter

Peasant woman

Merchant

Farmer

Becoming a knight

Knights were generally of noble birth. They had to leave their family at a young age, because a knight's training involved many years' work. The young gentleman had to learn to ride, fight and serve his lord before he was ready to become a knight.

From page to squire

At the age of seven, the boy left home to join a nobleman's household. This meant living in a castle and serving the whole family as a page. The young man was taught how to act politely, as well as learning to ride and handle weapons. When he was about 14 years old, a successful page became a squire. Then his duties were to serve a knight, looking after his master's horses, armour and weapons. Eventually he rode into battle with his knight.

Children playing a board game

▲ A page is waiting to serve drinks to the ladies of the castle. The page has been taught that it is good manners to wait until he is called.

◄ This Frenchman is being knighted by his lord (see opposite), who holds the sword high with great ceremony. A line of trumpeters announces the importance of the event.

Page, sent with goblets of drink from the kitchen

Tapestries were popular for decoration and showed off the owner's wealth. They also helped to insulate the cold, stone walls

Sconce (wall bracket) holds a candle or flaming light

Noblewomen and nuns did a lot of embroidery as a pleasant and useful pastime

Lady writing

Lady checks the linen in the linen chest

Lute, a popular medieval musical instrument

Dogs, such as Irish wolfhounds, were kept to help with hunting, but some became pets

Rushes on the stone floor

Hobby horse, for children to pretend to ride

Knighthood

When an experienced squire was about 20, he could become a knight. If he did especially well in battle, he might be made a knight on the battlefield. Usually, however, this important occasion was marked by a special ceremony. It began with a ceremonial bath, followed by a night of prayer. Next day, a crowd watched as he received his sword and spurs. Then he knelt before an experienced knight, his master and sometimes even the king, who tapped him on the shoulder with his own sword and dubbed him a knight. Sometimes the ceremony was followed by a tournament (see page 22), where the new knight could show off his skills.

Dress like a knight

Early knights protected their bodies in battle with chain mail coats, which were made up of lots of small, linked iron rings. From the 14th century, knights began to add steel plates to their chain mail to protect their limbs and a coat of plates to protect their bodies. This project shows you how to make a cloak and breastplate.

Dress like a knight in your ▼ breastplate and cloak. Find out how to make a knight's sword and shield on pages 16–17.

Find out how to make a knight's pennant on pages 24–25

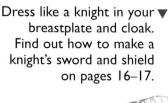

Protect your head in combat. Instructions to make the helmet are on pages 12–13

Knights would have put on a cloak to keep warm in cold weather. But they would not have worn one in battle – a cloak would get in the way when fighting

A knight's cloak

1

Cut out a piece of fabric 120 x 120cm. Ask an adult to trim the edges with pinking shears so they will not fray. Fold one edge of the fabric 6-8cm to make a tube and pin it in place. Spread strong fabric glue along the bottom of the tube to hold it in place. Leave to dry and remove the pins. Thread ribbon through the tube, gathering as you go.

You will need

- Thick fabric
- Tape measure
- Pinking shears
- Silver foil
- Black cord
- Hole punch
- Poster paints
- Wide ribbon
- Thin cardboard
- Paper fasteners
- Thick cardboard
- Sticky tape
- Scissors
- Pins
- Fabric glue
- Glue
- Paintbrush

A knight's breastplate

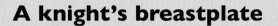

1

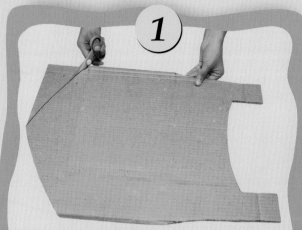

Cut two breastplate shapes from thick card, following the design shown above. These shapes should be the size to fit your body. Then cut two shoulder straps from strips of card, each measuring about 5cm x 40cm.

2

Cover the straps and the breastplate shape with silver foil, then glue on the straps. An adult can help you to adjust the straps to fit your body before you glue them in place.

Push paper fasteners through holes along the neck and armholes, to look like metal rivets. Bend back the 'arms' of the fasteners and glue them into position or cover them with tape.

3

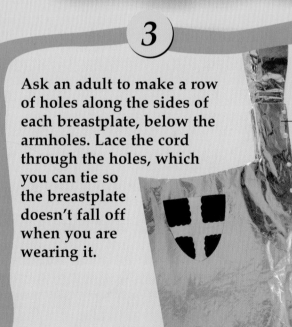

Ask an adult to make a row of holes along the sides of each breastplate, below the armholes. Lace the cord through the holes, which you can tie so the breastplate doesn't fall off when you are wearing it.

Design a coat of arms for the front of ▶ your breastplate on a sheet of paper or thin card, and glue it in place.

Clothing and armour

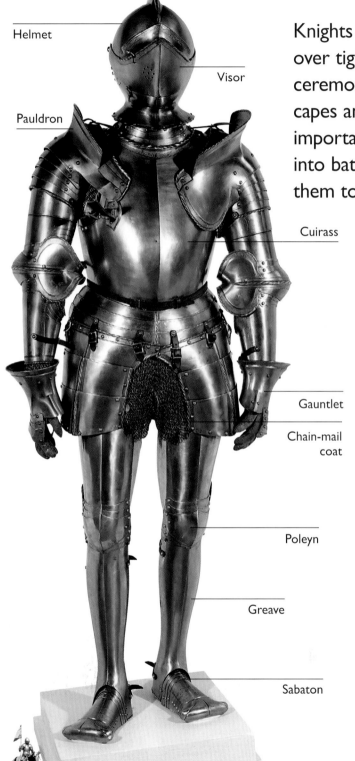

Helmet

Visor

Pauldron

Cuirass

Gauntlet

Chain-mail coat

Poleyn

Greave

Sabaton

Knights often wore colourful surcoats over tight-fitting tunics and breeches. For ceremonial occasions, they added fur-lined capes and jewelled felt hats. But much more important to them was the armour they wore into battle. This armoured defence allowed them to concentrate on all-out attack.

Mail and plate

Most knights rode into battle in full body armour. Over a padded jacket they wore a long coat made of chain mail (interlaced iron rings). This flexible armour, called a hauberk, gave the body overall protection. A strong metal helmet (see page 12) protected the knight's head. In later times, separate strips of metal plate were worn over the hauberk. By about 1400, the plates were joined together to make a complete suit of hard armour.

◀ This suit of armour may have belonged to the famous French knight, Chevalier Bayard (1475–1524). Each plate was specially shaped to protect a particular part of the body and had its own name.

Helmet

Chain-mail collar, protecting neck

Surcoat worn over chain-mail armour

Sheathed sword

Rowl spur, with spiked wheel

Lance with banner attached, showing a cross

Shield with a cross ordinary, carried by Crusader knights

This section of stained ▶ glass from a church shows a Christian knight in armour.

Coats of arms

The knight's strong wooden shield usually displayed an emblem so that he could be recognized. This was useful in the heat of battle, to tell friend from foe, and also helped identify the most successful warriors. The emblem, known as a coat of arms, was chosen from a series of well-known designs. By the 13th century, coats of arms were also common in civilian life. They were widely used by noblemen to identify their family, and the individual design was passed on from generation to generation. When they married, a husband and wife could combine their emblems to create a new coat of arms.

◀ Some basic designs for shields. They were called ordinaries, and each one had a special name.

Pall   Pile   Cross   Saltire

Make a knight's helmet

Warriors first started wearing helmets to protect their heads during the Bronze Age. Helmets were also worn by the Ancient Greeks and Romans. In the Middle Ages, helmets became larger, for extra protection for the head and neck. This project shows you how to make a helm – an early type of helmet that completely enclosed the head.

Head cases

Early helmets, called helms, were shaped like cylinders. Although padded inside, they would have been extremely uncomfortable. The basinet became popular during the 1300s. Basinets had a pig-shaped snout, studded with holes for breathing. The close-helmet was rounded to fit the wearer's head and had a visor at the front to protect the face.

▼ A strong helmet was vital to protect the knight's head from a sword blow or an arrow.

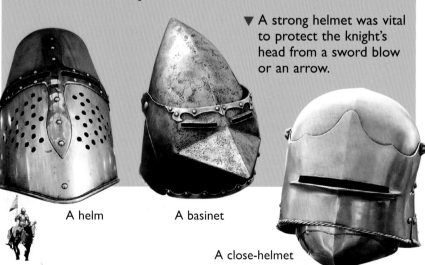

A helm   A basinet

A close-helmet

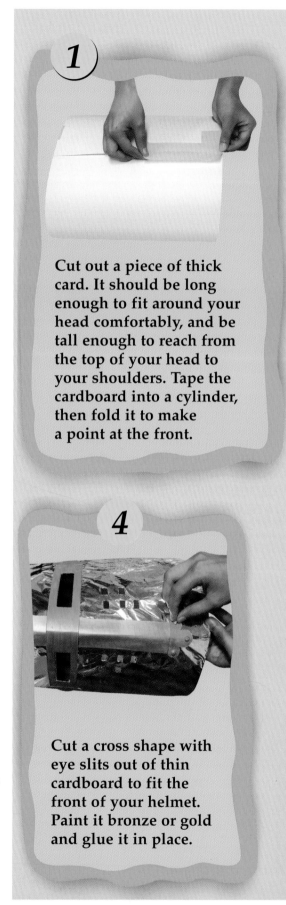

1

Cut out a piece of thick card. It should be long enough to fit around your head comfortably, and be tall enough to reach from the top of your head to your shoulders. Tape the cardboard into a cylinder, then fold it to make a point at the front.

4

Cut a cross shape with eye slits out of thin cardboard to fit the front of your helmet. Paint it bronze or gold and glue it in place.

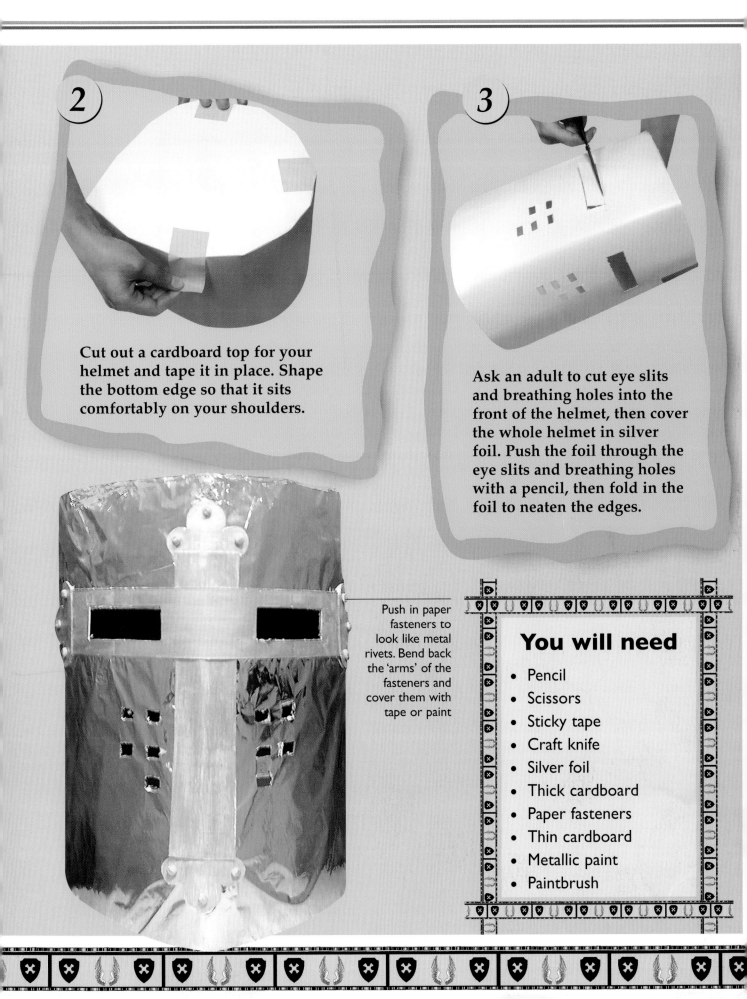

2

Cut out a cardboard top for your helmet and tape it in place. Shape the bottom edge so that it sits comfortably on your shoulders.

3

Ask an adult to cut eye slits and breathing holes into the front of the helmet, then cover the whole helmet in silver foil. Push the foil through the eye slits and breathing holes with a pencil, then fold in the foil to neaten the edges.

Push in paper fasteners to look like metal rivets. Bend back the 'arms' of the fasteners and cover them with tape or paint

You will need

- Pencil
- Scissors
- Sticky tape
- Craft knife
- Silver foil
- Thick cardboard
- Paper fasteners
- Thin cardboard
- Metallic paint
- Paintbrush

Weapons

A knight had to provide his own weapons. He also had to look after them, and his squire helped keep them clean and in good order. There were various different kinds of arms, most of which were specially developed for close combat on horseback.

First line of attack

Charging into battle, the knight's first weapon of attack was his lance. This was a strong wooden spear, up to three metres long, with a tip of iron or steel. The knight carried the lance under his arm, and in later times he had a special bracket attached to his breastplate, which made it easier to control the weapon. The aim was to strike an opponent and knock him off his horse.

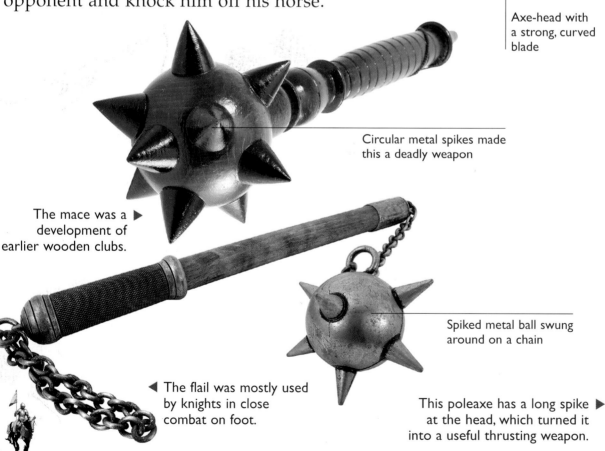

Axe-head with a strong, curved blade

Circular metal spikes made this a deadly weapon

The mace was a ▶ development of earlier wooden clubs.

Spiked metal ball swung around on a chain

◀ The flail was mostly used by knights in close combat on foot.

This poleaxe has a long spike ▶ at the head, which turned it into a useful thrusting weapon.

▲ The Battle of Neville's Cross, in 1346.
English knights and archers defeated the
Scots, who were allies of the French.

Knights wield poleaxes
and maces in a mêlée

Mounted knights fight
hand to hand with swords

Poleaxe, mace and flail

When it came to closer combat, the knight's
favourite weapon was his sword (see page 16).
This was so important that it became a symbol
of knighthood. If possible, a knight used the
same sword throughout his life. But there
were other devastating close-combat weapons.

The poleaxe had a wooden shaft, sometimes
sheathed in iron and nearly two metres long,
which was wielded with both hands. Injury to an
opponent was done by the cutting blade of the
axe, the hammerhead club on the other side, or
a long metal spike at the end. The mace and flail
were both swung around to inflict terrible
injuries to enemies.

Make a sword and shield

A knight used different weapons in combat, such as a lance, mace and axe. But his most important weapon – and a symbol of knighthood itself – was his sword. Follow the steps to make your own sword and a shield.

Knightly swords

Up until the late 1200s, most knights used double-edge cutting swords in battle. However, as plate armour became more popular, swordsmiths developed more pointed swords, which could be thrust through the gaps between the plates of a knight's armour. From the 14th century, larger versions of ordinary swords were developed. These great, two-hand swords were so-called because they needed both hands to swing them.

◀ Knights sometimes carried a two-hand sword like this into battle, hung from their saddle, as well as their ordinary sword.

Sword

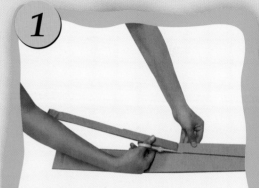

Cut two pointed, sword blade shapes from corrugated card. They should measure about 90cm long and 6cm at the widest point.

Shield

Cut two shield shapes out of corrugated cardboard. Cut a slot measuring 14 x 3cm in the centre of one shield.

2

Score down the centre of the length of each blade using a pen top and ruler. Then fold slightly to make a ridge. Glue the blades back to back, so the ridges are on the outside. Cover with silver foil.

3

Crossguard

Cut a strip of thin card 22 x 14cm. Fold it in half lengthways and cut a slit in the centre of the fold. Then slide the blade through the slit to make a crossguard.

4

Shaped crossguard

Pommel

Shape the crossguard and glue on a card pommel at the top of the hilt. Paint both gold. Wind black tape around the handle and glue on a plastic jewel.

2

Cut out a long strip of card measuring 28 x 2.5–2.75cm to make the shield's handle. Fold it in half and glue or tape it over the slot.

You will need

- Thin cardboard
- Scissors
- Metallic paints
- Poster paints
- Paintbrushes
- Corrugated cardboard
- Plastic 'jewel'
- White emulsion paint
- Silver foil
- Glue
- Black tape
- Scissors

3

Glue the two shield shapes together. Cover the shield in a coat of white emulsion before painting with colour poster paints.

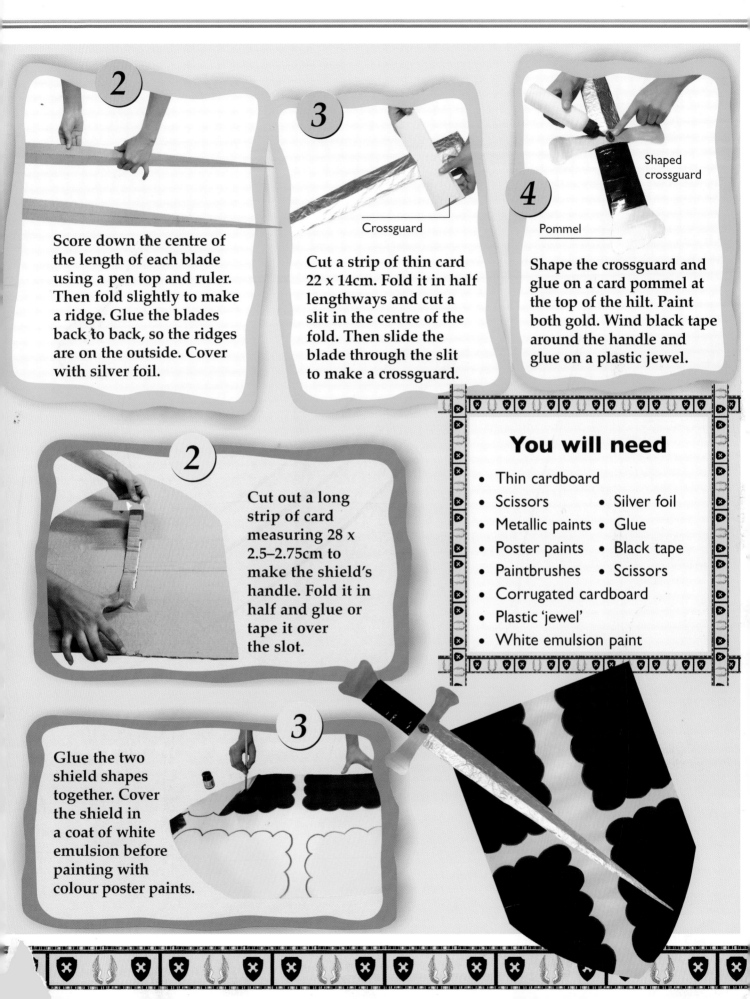

Castles

When they were not away fighting battles, many knights lived in castles. These were stone fortresses, built by kings and noblemen to defend their land and households. Castles were built for living in, as well as for defence.

Built for protection

A castle's main building was the tall stone keep, which contained the lord's private apartments, sleeping quarters and a chapel. Outside was a courtyard, called a bailey, surrounded by high stone walls. Large castles had another area beyond the walls, called an outer bailey, with a second surrounding wall. Further protection was provided by a deep moat around the whole castle. The single entrance was approached by crossing a drawbridge across the moat, which could be raised into the gatehouse for security.

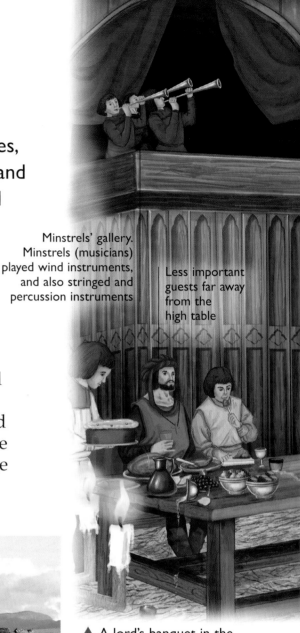

Minstrels' gallery. Minstrels (musicians) played wind instruments, and also stringed and percussion instruments

Less important guests far away from the high table

▲ A lord's banquet in the great hall was a splendid affair. The owner of a castle liked to entertain his guests in style.

◄ Harlech Castle, in North Wales, built for King Edward I of England between 1283 and 1290. It once survived a seven-year siege and later became the family home of Welsh prince Owain Glyndwr.

Sconce

Page serving
roast pig

Jester juggling
and providing
entertainment

Lord, lady and
chief guests

High table, on a
raised platform
called a dais

Trencher — large
piece of stale
bread used
as a plate

In the great hall

The castle's largest room was the great hall, which was usually separate from the keep. This room was for meals, meetings and sometimes for sleeping. There was a kitchen and food store at one end of the great hall and private apartments at the other. Important guests were entertained in the great hall, often with splendid banquets. The lord of the castle, his lady and their chief guests sat at a raised, high table. Other diners sat at a lower level, on benches at long trestle tables, enjoying a huge feast of meats, such as venison, boar and goose. While they ate, which they mostly did with their fingers, they were entertained by minstrels and jesters.

Play Fox and Geese

In the evenings, a knight might spend his time dancing, or listening to poetry or songs performed by strolling players or musicians who travelled from castle to castle. People also enjoyed playing games, such as blind man's buff and bowling. Here is how to play a board game for two players called Fox and Geese, which was very popular during the Middle Ages.

Fun and games

Popular games in the Middle Ages included marbles, dice, knucklebones and board games, such as draughts and chess. Playing cards with four suits and court cards (kings, queens and jacks) spread from the Islamic world to Europe by the early 14th century. The first cards were hand-painted and only the very wealthy could afford them.

▲ These chessmen, dating from the Middle Ages, have been carved from walrus ivory and whales' teeth. They were found on the Isle of Lewis, off north-west Scotland.

Copy the plan of the board onto a sheet of white paper or card. It is made up of five squares. Each square has lines that cross each other. Use a ruler and pencil to get the lines straight and even.

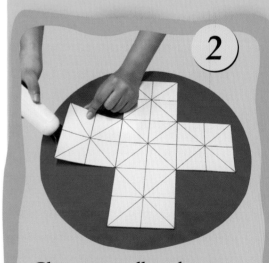

Glue your cardboard cross on to a large circle of red card mounted on a piece of thick, corrugated card.

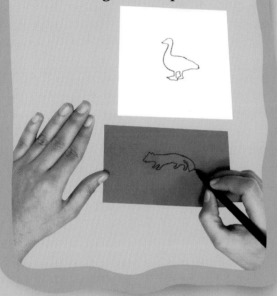

3

Make some counters out of white and red cardboard. You need 13 white geese and one red fox. If you like, cut them into fox or geese shapes.

You can play the game using small ▼ plastic counters instead of card shapes – but make sure you have one colour for the fox, and another colour for the geese!

Starting position for a game of Fox and Geese, with the fox in the centre of the board

How to play

There are several ways of playing Fox and Geese. In these rules, there are 13 geese and one fox. The fox wins by capturing enough geese so that they cannot trap him. The geese win if they can crowd the fox into a corner so that he cannot move.

Place the counters on the board as shown in the picture below, with the fox in the centre and the geese at one side of the board.

Take turns to be the fox or the geese – you can decide by tossing a coin or throwing the dice. Each player takes turns to move, one counter at a time. The geese move first.

Geese can only move directly forwards, diagonally forwards or sideways, to the next spot.

The fox can move forwards, backwards or sideways to an empty point. The fox may also jump over a goose if there is an empty point behind it. It then captures the goose and removes it from the board for the rest of the game.

The fox can jump over two or more geese at a time, capturing all of them, if there are empty points behind each one.

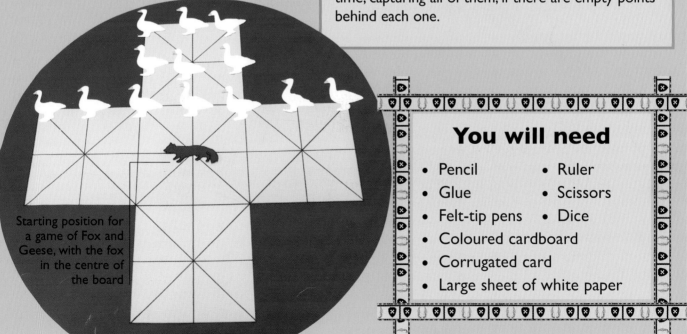

You will need

- Pencil
- Glue
- Felt-tip pens
- Coloured cardboard
- Corrugated card
- Large sheet of white paper
- Ruler
- Scissors
- Dice

Tournaments

Early tournaments were mock battles between two large teams of knights. They were useful for military training and exercise. By the 13th century, individual jousting had become more popular as a form of sport and entertainment for the watching crowds.

Jousting

Jousts were held in an enclosed area of land called the lists. A joust was a form of single combat with lances, but the weapons were usually blunted at the end so that it was more of a sport than a life-or-death duel. Two knights charged at each other and tried to knock their opponent off his horse with a strong, direct hit on his shield. If a lance was broken three times, the contest continued on foot and the knights fought with swords.

A joust being fought on an ▶ 'Italian course', which means that the knights are separated by a wooden barrier. The horses are dressed both for protection and to identify their riders.

◀ Ladies in the stand watch a fierce mock battle as part of an early tournament. This was for practice and entertainment, but there were often serious injuries.

Coronel lance tip
(rounded)

Covered stand

Vamplate,
protecting the
knight's hand

Coat of arms of the
lord and lady of
the Tournament

Lance

Banner of a
contestant

Crinet (horse's
neck armour)

Shaffron (horse's face armour)

Wooden
barrier

Queen of the tournament

Only knights could take part in tournaments, and before the event they usually displayed banners or pennants with their coat of arms, to show who they were. The ladies who attended the tournament as spectators chose one of the contestants, a 'knight of honour', to open the event. Then one of the ladies was herself chosen to preside over the festivities as Queen of the tournament (or Queen of Beauty). She was given a seat of honour in the stand and, most importantly, was given the opportunity to award a prize to the victorious knight. In some very large tournaments, a new Queen of Beauty was chosen every day.

Make some pennants

At every tournament, knights displayed banners showing their coats of arms and other designs. Some knights had special banner-bearers to carry their colours. This project shows you how to make a simple, triangular pennant and decorate it with a coat of arms.

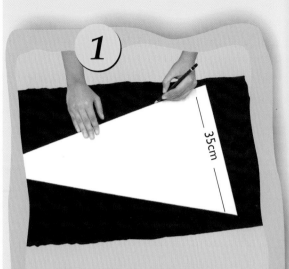

Cut out a template and use it to cut out a long thin triangle of fabric. The triangle's short, straight edge should measure around 35cm.

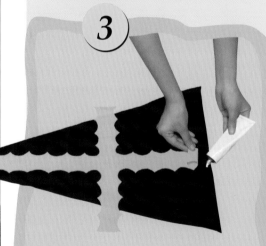

Glue on your shapes with fabric glue and, if necessary, trim them to fit.

Heraldic banners

Knights often carried long flags on the tips of their lances, to help identify each other at a tournament, or in battle. These flags, called pennons, usually had long forked tails, and displayed the owner's coat of arms. Many knights also displayed their arms on large, square banners. The size of a banner was usually a sign of the owner's rank, so a king's banner was larger than that of a lord, and a lord's larger than a knight's. Another type of flag, the standard, displayed heraldic devices to help to identify the owner such as a badge, or a motto.

Knights in the late 11th century set off for battle with their banners and shields.

2

Cut shapes out of cloth to decorate your pennant.

You will need

- Strong glue   • Scissors
- Corrugated cardboard
- Fabric (in different colours)
- Metallic paint
- Wooden broom handle
- Thin white cardboard
- Fabric glue

▼ If you want to make a repeat pattern, such as the fleur de lys (left), it is easier to make a card template first. Then you can trace around it on to the cloth, so that all your cloth pieces are the same size.

Use fabric glue to stick the cut-out fabric shapes in place

4

You could paint the broom handles in metallic paint, too.

Cut out two pieces of cardboard in the shape of a leaf to decorate the top of the broom handle. Glue them together. When dry, paint in gold, bronze or silver metallic paint. Glue the cardboard top and the flag to the broom handle.

Knightly orders

Knights formed groups called orders. The members of an order vowed loyalty to their lord or king and worked together to protect him and defend his lands. Some of the most famous orders were the religious groups formed during the Crusades.

Hospitallers, Templars and Teutonic knights

The Hospitallers were members of the Order of the Hospital of St John of Jerusalem. They ran a monastery and hospital dedicated to St John the Baptist, and wore a black habit with a white cross. By about 1150, they had also become a military order. The Knights Templar were originally protectors of the site of the Temple of Solomon in Jerusalem. The Teutonic Knights were a German order, whose members turned their attentions from the Holy Land to central Europe.

Hospitaller knight

Templar knight

Teutonic knight

▲ The most famous three Christian military orders all wore the cross on their surcoat and shield.

▲ Krak des Chevaliers, a 12th-century crusader castle built in Syria by Hospitaller knights.

Templar and Teutonic banners

Templar knight Guillaume de Clermont, wielding a mace

Saracen (Muslim warrior) with round shield

Siege ladder

Towered walls surrounding the city of Acre

▶ A 19th-century French painting of the Siege of Acre. Crusaders lost the city of Acre, capital and final stronghold of the Kingdom of Jerusalem, in 1291. After a six-week siege, Muslim warriors overpowered the Christian knights.

The Crusades

The Crusades (or Wars of the Cross, 1096–1291) were a series of military expeditions by Christian knights to recover their Holy Land from Muslims. Many thousands of knights set out on the First Crusade in 1096, which was called for by Pope Urban II, and they succeeded in capturing Jerusalem from the Saracens in 1099.

They then set up four states, which the knights ruled from a chain of castles. Knightly orders became more religious as a result, but individual knights took the opportunity to make their fortunes by seizing land and treasure. By the end of the 13th century, the Muslim warriors had become more powerful and Christian knights lost their holy war in the Middle East. Their last stronghold was Acre, in modern Israel.

Make a jewelled chalice

Most countries in Western Europe were Roman Catholic until the 16th century, and the Church played a big part in people's everyday lives. This project shows you how to make a chalice, a kind of cup used to hold wine during Mass, the main Roman Catholic service. Many chalices were richly decorated and showed the importance and wealth of the Church.

Knight at prayer

Some knights became monks after living a life of violence, as they believed that this would make it easier for them to enter heaven after they died. Many knights went on pilgrimages to shrines, to pray for help from saints.

A 12th-century English ▶ knight at prayer. Some historians think this picture may represent King Henry III of England (1216–1272). This illustration is a 19th-century engraving.

1

Cover just over half of a balloon with overlapping torn strips of newspaper covered in wallpaper paste. Do four or five layers, then leave until completely dry.

4

Tape the base, stem and bowl together, then add three to four layers of newspaper strips soaked in wallpaper paste to secure them.

2

Pop the balloon. Cut out a bowl shape from the papier-mâché. Glue strips of newspaper around the rim to neaten the edge.

You will need

- Cardboard
- Glue
- String
- Metallic paint
- Newspaper
- Wallpaper paste
- Cardboard tube (for example, from a paper towel roll)
- Paintbrush
- Scissors
- Plastic jewels
- Balloon
- Sticky tape

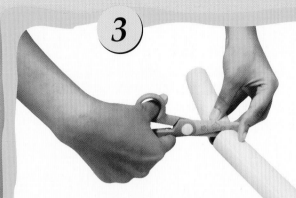

3

Cut down a card tube to make the chalice's stem. Make a base from a circle of card by cutting a slit from the edge of the card to the centre then curving it into a cone shape.

Make a cone-shaped base from card

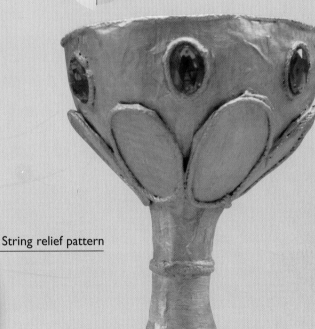

String relief pattern

5

Glue on a relief pattern in string, then paint the chalice in gold or silver metallic paint, and add some shiny, plastic jewels.

Timeline

1066 Normans conquer England; William the Conqueror builds castles to defend his new realm.

1095 Pope Urban II calls for the First Crusade to recapture the Christian Holy Land.

1096–99 First Crusade, led by famous knights Godfrey of Bouillon, Raymond of Toulouse, Robert of Flanders and Bohemond of Taranto.

1099 Crusader knights capture Jerusalem from Muslims.

1113 Pope Paschal II recognizes the Hospitallers as a religious order (Knights of St John of Jerusalem).

1119 The Templars order is founded in Jerusalem by the French knights Hugh des Payens and Godfrey of St Omer.

1146–1219 Life of William Marshal, Earl of Pembroke, a famous knight known for his loyalty to the crown.

1190 Foundation of the order of Teutonic Knights (of the Hospital of St Mary the Virgin).

1192 After many great battles, Richard I (the Lionheart) of England reaches a truce with the great Muslim warrior Saladin.

1204 Knights of the Fourth Crusade sack Constantinople.

1228–29 Holy Roman Emperor Frederick II leads the Sixth Crusade.

1244 Muslims retake Jerusalem from Crusaders.

1270 Eighth (and last) Crusade by Christian knights against the Muslims.

1272–1307 Reign of Edward I of England, who builds many great castles.

1292 Edward I introduces laws banning pointed lances and sharp swords in tournaments.

1337–1453 The Hundred Years War between England and France.

1346 English defeat French at the Battle of Crécy, with 1500 French knights killed.

1347 Order of the Garter founded by Edward III (reigned 1327–77).

1382–1439 Life of Richard Beauchamp, Earl of Warwick, a famous Knight of the Bath and of the Garter.

1475–1524 Life of Chevalier Bayard, known as the model of a chivalrous knight.

Glossary

bailey The courtyard of a castle.

charger A strong, fast horse.

chivalry An honourable code of conduct followed by medieval knights.

coat of arms An emblem standing for a person or family.

Crusades Military expeditions by Christian knights to recover areas of the Holy Land captured by Muslim warriors.

destrier A knight's large warhorse.

flail A club with a free-swinging metal ball attached.

Holy Land The historic region of Palestine, holy to Christians, Jews and Muslims.

jester An entertainer employed to amuse by juggling and acting the fool.

keep The innermost fortified part of a castle.

mace A heavy club with a metal head.

mêlée A mass hand-to-hand battle.

Middle Ages The period between ancient and modern times (AD 500–1500), also known as the Medieval period.

minstrel A musician, singer or reciter of poetry.

moat A water-filled ditch around a castle.

nobleman A high-ranking man of noble birth, such as a baron.

ordinary A basic design painted on a shield.

page A youth acting as a personal or household servant.

palfrey A light horse ridden for hunting and long-distance travel.

poleaxe A weapon with an axe on a long pole.

Saracen A Muslim warrior of the Middle Ages.

spur A spike or spiked wheel worn on a rider's heel to make a horse go faster.

squire A young man acting as an attendant to a knight.

sumpter A packhorse.

surcoat A coat worn over armour.

venison The meat of a deer.

visor The hinged part of a helmet that can be opened.

Index

Webfinder

www.castles.me.uk
Learn more about British medieval castles and knights.

www.cybrary.org/medieval.htm
Lots of information about knights, castles and the Middle Ages.

www.knightsandarmor.com/index.htm
All about the history of medieval knights.

www.medievalcrusades.com
All about the Christian Crusades.

www.metmuseum.org/explore/knights/title.html
A look at arms and armour, including a Joust Challenge game.

MAKING HISTORY

SERIES CONTENTS